Live and Learn or Learn and Live:

What to Do When You Go to College

A brutally honest account of my mistakes in college

by

Benjamin Lee

Table of Contents

Page

Introduction

I heard a preacher once say, "Someone is preying for you." Notice that the word is not *praying* but *preying*. There is someone preying for you. I'm referring to the devil, 1 Peter 5:8.

The devil is alive, well, and on a mission to destroy my life and yours. When we look around in our society, we can see the devil's fingerprints in many places. He has been busy and sadly is often successful. One of the most dangerous periods in one's life where the devil is active is during the college years. This is when many young people leave mom and dad for the first time. They have freedom like never before. They also have hundreds of ungodly and unrighteous peers attempting to influence them.

The reason why I know this is true is because I lived it. I am not proud of many things I did while I was in college. This is exactly why I wrote this short book for you. I want you to know about the dangers you will face in college. I want you to know what to do *and not do* when you begin your collegiate life.

What are you supposed to do when you go to college? Serve God. He wants you to seek Him first, Matthew 6:33. But the devil is also hoping that you will serve him. He has a plan for you, 2 Timothy 2:26. Hopefully, my story and tips will aid you in making the right decisions. Ultimately, you need to listen to God's word. It's better to learn and live instead of living and learning. God's word is always going to lead you in the right direction. You need it. We all need it, Jeremiah 10:23. No matter how smart you are or how smart you think you are, God knows what is best.

I originally wrote this in 2010. I've decided to get this to as many young people as possible because I want them to be successful. It can be hard for Christians to admit their mistakes. But we all make mistakes. The apostle Paul often rehearsed many of the mistakes he made, 1 Timothy 1:13. My desire to write this is not to brag or for people to think I have all the answers, but rather to help young people think during those decisive moments that can have a ripple effect for many years. May God be with you. Remember, Jesus loves you. At the end of this book are some additional thoughts from Steven Estes, Keith Stonehart, and Doy Moyer. I thank these men for their faith and concern for young people.

Chapter One:
Good Intentions Not Good Enough

I was thrilled to go to college in 1996. My mother and father never attended college. For years, I went to Fighting Illini football and basketball games at the University of Illinois. Now, I was about to become a Fighting Illini. I had the best of both worlds. I was able to stay in my hometown and go to a top tier school.

Looking back on those days, I see how blessed I was. I developed a strong work ethic from my mother (my father was not around), and through her example, I was determined to do well in high school. That hard work paid off in numerous scholarships. I ended up with some student loans, but I had everything covered. My mother didn't have to pay out of pocket for tuition, room, and board, or for my books. YES!

But it got even better. I was going to room with my best friend at the time, who was a fellow brother in Christ. I couldn't ask for much more. As I began to get ready for school, I had good intentions to make an impact on campus for good. I was diligent about expressing my faith throughout high school. People knew where I stood on issues, like drinking and smoking. Now I was going to help those poor souls on campus.

I began school shortly after moving into our dorm. It was a private dorm, which simply means it was more expensive than a regular dorm. My roommate and I shared one bathroom with the room next to ours. We signed up for this because it was much better than sharing a bathroom with an entire floor.

Not only did I have good intentions about helping people coming to Christ, but I also intended to have a perfect GPA. These intentions began to fall apart quickly. I took 12 hours my first semester and ended up with a 2.7/GPA. That's bad, right? I almost failed Geology 101. How dumb could I have been? I was putting in the study time I thought I needed. I realized that studying in college is much different compared to studying in high school. Thankfully, I ended up graduating with a 3.2/GPA. Unfortunately, as my grades improved, my morals declined.

College was like nothing I had seen before. I had good intentions to live a godly life, but I was not prepared at all. I had grown up in a church with only about 5–10 members. We had no teen classes. We had no vacation Bible school. Not having some type of connection with other young people who were striving to do the right thing, in the long run, had a big impact. I was more prone to be persuaded in crucial situations, rather than being the leader God wanted me to be. Yes, I had a Christian roommate, but that didn't do any good because we both ended up being negative influences on each other. Good intentions are not good enough.

Read 1 Samuel 13:1-13. King Saul had instructions from the prophet Samuel. Yet King Saul wouldn't listen. Saul had good intentions but his good intentions were not good enough. What can you learn from King Saul?

_____

_____

_____

_____

_____

Questions

1. Do your Christian friends outnumber your non-Christian friends? YES/NO. If they don't, in what way do you think this will affect you in school?

2. What are your intentions when you go to college? How many of those intentions are spiritual in nature?

3. Have you thought about the drastic changes you will face in college? YES/NO. What are some of the biggest changes that might be a temptation to you? What plans do you have in place to overcome temptation?

What to Do

When you begin your college life:

1. You need to determine that you are going to be a leader and not a follower.

2. You need to spend as much time as possible with Christian friends. Even when you go to school, keep in touch with your godly friends from high school.

3. You need to know where you will be worshipping before school begins. Have a plan. Finding a congregation should play a big factor with where you go to school. Having to travel an hour or so to attend services may be difficult. Set yourself up not just for scholastic success but also spiritual success. Be sure to also set spiritual goals.

4. Your classes will be different. It would be wise to get a tutor or take fewer hours the first semester to get comfortable with your workload.

_____

_____

One thing that woke me up and prompted me to change was seeing my father ruin his life largely due to drinking. My dad married a great woman (my mom). He had a great job, a great place to live, and a couple of cars. But it was drinking that played a big role in his downfall. He began to drink socially when he was in a bowling club. This social drinking gradually increased to drinking on a regular basis. My dad was a good person when he was sober. But he was a totally different person when he was drunk. He would curse, fight, and at times hit my mother. I refused to be like him. But the most important reason drinking is so stupid, is because it's wrong in the sight of God.

The Bible says a lot about drunkenness and how this will keep us out of the kingdom of God, 1 Corinthians 6:9-11. Wait, I know what you're thinking. You're probably saying, "Well, as long as I don't get drunk, it's no big deal. I will just have a few beers." WRONG, MY FRIEND! Trust me, when I say that peer pressure will get the best of you. But consider this also for a moment. Why would God condemn getting drunk but then allow us to go down the path that's going to take us to that final destination? It's poor logic when people attempt to say a few drinks are okay. Why even begin the process of becoming drunk? Here's what I know. My dad, before he died at the young age of 59, wasn't looking for another drink. Going to those fraternity parties was what got me drinking. I thank God I have been able to overcome drinking.

Questions

1. Have you ever consumed alcohol? YES/NO
2. Have you ever tried to justify why you should drink? YES/NO If so, how have you justified it?
3. Do you plan on drinking in college? YES/NO
4. What are you going to tell people when they want you to go out and drink?
5. If you've said yes to any of these, go back and reread those scriptures I mentioned earlier. What does God want you to know? Learn and live!

What to Do

When the parties begin:

- Fraternity and sorority parties are usually from Thursday through Sunday (although I was in school a long time ago). Make sure you have something scheduled during these times if they are a temptation for you.

- Set your standards high. Let others know where you stand on this issue. Then stand fast in your faith.
- Spend time with like-minded people that will help you to stick to your beliefs.
- You may need to get off campus on the weekends to avoid parties.
- If there are no college devotions with the local congregations, then start one. Friday night is a great night to have them.
- You can still have fun and not drink. Go bowling, workout, see a movie, play mini-golf, go out to eat, etc.
- Study why it's wrong to drink so you will be firm on your beliefs and answers. Remember God's word is always right.

Chapter Three:
Sex, Sex, Sex

Whether you're a young man or woman, going to school, I think the biggest temptation you will face will be sexual immorality. I have never used drugs. I never cheated when I was in college. However, I did fall short of the glory of God when it came to sexual immorality. The Bible says so much about avoiding sexual immorality. Read 1 Thessalonians 4:1-5. What do you learn from this passage?

_____

_____

_____

_____

The devil is very cunning. He doesn't want us to think what Paul said to the church in Thessalonica is true. Our society is focused on SEX. Everywhere you look from movies to music, sex is being thrown in our faces. The sexual relationship is designed for marriage. It is to be enjoyed in marriage. It is for husband and wife, Genesis 2:22-25; Proverbs 5:15-19.

When I began my freshmen year, I was a virgin. I was proud of that fact, at least at the beginning. However, I was totally different than the majority of the students on campus. This became evident as soon as I moved into my dorm. I lived in a coed dorm. There were men and women on the same floor. I quickly saw how the guys had their girlfriends over in their dorm rooms, and it wasn't to study. After a while, this became normal for me to see and eventually to do. One of my buddies would often talk about the girls he had sex with. This was not something I needed to hear. In fact, if I was smart about it, I would have left the dorm at the end of the semester and moved back home, where I wouldn't be around the constant temptation.

As my college years went by, maintaining purity became increasingly more difficult. While I was still a virgin, I was engaging in behavior I should not have. While I was not engaging in intercourse, I was doing everything else like passionate kissing and touching. Some people may refer to this as getting to first or second base, but it really is foreplay. It is behavior designed for a man and woman in marriage. When people do this, they are setting themselves up for failure.

I was deceiving myself into thinking that as long as I didn't go all the way, I was okay. But I was wrong.

Read Proverbs 6:27-28. What does it say? Read it closely. Write out the passage below.

_____

_____

_____

_____

_____

I graduated from college in 2000. It was during that year I lost my virginity. I lost the special gift:

- God wanted me to give to my wife.
- You can never get back no matter what you do.

I lost this special gift with whom I thought I loved. But I really lusted after her. We would eventually break up, which was devastating. When we broke up over the phone, she said, "Go find a Christian girl to be with…" I had been a sellout when it came to my faith. I lost a precious gift. Don't live and learn. It will come with a price. Learn and live.

Sometimes, I don't think young people think about their actions and the consequences that are attached. I sure didn't. I had avoided sex for so long. However, throughout my college years, I was playing with fire. You can only play with fire for so long before you get burned. As I said before, God is always right. It pays to listen to Him. But I was not thinking about how this would affect me years down the road when I went looking for a spouse. I now had one less thing I could offer my future spouse. I now had to worry about whether or not my girlfriend was going to get pregnant, or if she had an STD I didn't know about. During that time, I thought we were going to be together forever. Then when we broke up, it made it even more devastating because of what I had squandered in the heat of the moment. My friend, please learn and live, so you don't have to live and learn.

Questions

1. Are you a virgin? YES/NO

2. If YES, are you proud of being a virgin or embarrassed? Explain.

3. Do you plan on being a virgin until you get married? YES/NO. What steps will you need to take to ensure you will be able to overcome future temptations?

What to Do

To avoid sexual immorality:

- You must have the proper WHY.

  - It's not enough to say, "I will avoid sex because I don't want to get an STD." There are ways to reduce that threat.
  - It's not enough to say, "I don't want to get pregnant or get someone pregnant." One can use birth control or a condom to avoid this problem.
  - It's not enough to say, "I don't want my parents finding out." I hid a lot of things from my mother. You can hide things if you really want to.
  - Your WHY is found in 1 Peter 1:13-16. Be holy because God is holy. That should be your ultimate motivation.

- You must trust what God says to do, 1 Thessalonians 4:1-3. In fact, memorize this text.

- You must not deceive yourself into thinking you are strong enough to play with fire and not get burned.
- Avoid French kissing and maybe kissing altogether. Avoid touching. This will only cause you to want to do more.
- Go out with other couples to reduce the amount of temptations. No sleeping over in dorm rooms or apartments.
- Read your Bible and pray every single day.
- Date people (Christians) who have the same expectations you have. I made a major mistake by not dating Christians.
- Count the cost. Engaging in sex prior to marriage can and will affect your marriage. God wants you to be with one person for life.
- If you're watching porn, STOP! You will eventually do what you are watching. Get help and eliminate avenues you may be watching it through.

Chapter Four:
Fruity Fruit Punch

In high school, I ran cross-country and track. I was always active, and as a result, I kept my weight down. But during my freshman year, my worst nightmare became a reality. Many people had warned me about the freshman 15. This is the average amount of weight people gain their first year in college. I think there are various reasons for this:

- First, you are in a new environment. Most people don't like change. When change occurs, and we get out of our natural routine, we tend to overcompensate in one area or another. Food is one of these areas.
- Second, with classes and striving to get good grades, exercise seems to be put aside.
- Third, most college students begin to stay up late, and one of the things to do when you're up late is to eat.

Well, I gained about 15 pounds my freshman year. In my dorm, I only had one meal a day that was paid for, so I made sure I loaded up when I ate. One of the first things that caught my attention was the fruit punch machine. The first time I tried that red, sugary, fake punch, it was like a party for my taste buds. I couldn't get enough. The glasses the cafeteria had were extremely small, so I would get about 6–8 glasses of my favorite fruity fruit punch, and drink them all with a smile. It eventually showed up on my waist size. Before I knew it, I was getting fat. I continued down this path my sophomore and junior year. Thankfully, I began to get more serious with my health and weight in my junior year. I radically changed what I ate and when I ate, and before I knew it, the weight began to fall off. Take it from me; it's much easier to be consistent with your weight rather than having it bounce up and down. In fact, as Christians, we are to live lives of self-control, Galatians 5:22-23. We tend to overlook this command when it comes to eating. Your college years are preparing you for your future. Why do you want to begin your future overweight and unhealthy? This is not a good way to enter the workforce.

Questions

1. How many days a week are you currently exercising? If you're not exercising, why not?

2. Do you enjoy exercising? YES/NO. If you said no, then you are in for a big surprise with your weight in college.

3. On a scale of 1–10, with 10 being the best, how would you describe your current eating habits? If you answer below a 5, then you may want to speak to someone on campus or at a gym for some tips on how to eat better.

What to Do

To avoid weight gain in college:

- Eat breakfast.
- Drink plenty of water. Avoid sugary drinks like fruit punch, soda, coke, pop, or whatever you call it.
- MOVE, MOVE, MOVE. Walk or bike to classes and make time for exercise.
- Join a gym or a running club.
- Avoid eating late at night.
- Do cardio and lift weights.
- Give your stomach a break from time to time and fast. I typically try to fast about 10-12 hours from my last meal of the day to my first meal in the morning.

Chapter Five:
Pictures Never Go Away

I have a sense of humor. I think this is one of my great qualities. However, my sense of humor has caused me to do some pretty stupid things. To make matters worse, a camera has captured some of these stupid things. When I was in college, I did some silly things that I would not want anyone to see pictures of. They may have been funny then, but thinking back on it now, I can say I was pretty dumb.

The Internet has changed the world forever. Today, we can capture a moment and save it forever with a click of a button. We can upload a photo and allow the whole world to view it. You already know about all the different social media platforms that are out there. Photos have a way of lasting forever. I'm thankful we didn't have the social media apps we have today when I was in college.

You need to be aware of photos you take or that are taken of you. You must make sure you don't put yourself in a situation where someone could misconstrue something later. When I would go out to the bars, we would often take photos. These photos will never go away. When I went on spring break trips, we took tons of photos. Those last forever. Please don't misunderstand me. I'm not telling you to not take any pictures, so you can get away doing something wrong. I'm telling you to avoid sin altogether. When you do that, you will not have to worry about any photos.

Questions

1. Have you ever had a photo taken that you now regret? YES/NO.
2. What are some ways pictures you take in college could come back and haunt you later on in life?

What to Do

To avoid bad photos:

- Don't let total strangers take photos of you. You never know what they will do with them.
- Don't be in pictures where someone else is engaging in something you don't tolerate.
- When you're in pictures with people, make sure you are acting holy.
- Be covered up in the photos you take. You may be beautiful but dress appropriately.

Chapter Six:
Broke as a Joke

How much money did you get for graduating high school? Hopefully, you got some. Whether you received money as a gift or from your current job, chances are you entered your freshman year with some cash. But you may also graduate with a ton of debt. This seems to be the cycle so many college students follow. It was for me. I received a lot of cash when I graduated high school, but somehow ended up with around $15,000 worth of debt when I received my diploma.

Debt almost seems to be normal in our society. Athletes who are drafted will buy multiple homes and cars before they even get their first paycheck. They already owe people money before their first game. Families are living paycheck to paycheck. I believe many college students think it is normal to have a ton of school loans and credit card debt.

I began to set myself up for failure before my first class. I went to the quad day the university had every year prior to classes beginning. During that time, there were representatives from the clubs on campus. There were also credit card companies giving out free Tshirts and soda if you signed up for a card. I don't know if this is still happening today. Before I knew it, I had credit cards coming to me in the mail. I had never owned a credit card. I really didn't have a good grasp on how to handle money either. Growing up, we didn't talk much about money. When we did, it was always about how little money we had.

When I got my credit cards, I began to have some fun. Whatever the limit was on the cards, I got them to the max. I used them for spring break trips (bad idea). When I was in college, Circuit City was a really big deal. This was the place to buy electronics. I needed a stereo (or at least that's what I told myself), so I maxed out my Circuit City credit card. BOOM! It took me forever to pay it back. I was working part-time at Walgreens during college. I wasn't bringing in a lot of money. This was the beginning of a long line of mistakes with my finances.

I mentioned how I used my credit cards on spring break trips. My freshman year, I drove down to Daytona Beach with some friends. My first mistake was going to Daytona Beach. There was nothing down there for me except temptation, temptation, and temptation. I don't remember how much I spent on that trip, but it was a lot. It would take a while to repay all of that.

My sophomore year, I went to California with my sister. This was a fun trip, but again I didn't have the money. I charged a lot of stuff, and it took forever to pay back. My junior year I stayed at home (finally a good decision), but my senior year I was back to my old habits of making dumb decisions. This time I went to Jamaica.

Talk about making a huge mistake. First, I felt that since it was my senior year I deserved this trip. NOPE. WRONG. Second, I began working a night shift at FedEx to pay for the trip. This helped me out a little bit, but the majority of it was still charged to a credit card. I ended up paying for this trip for the next couple of years. Even worse than that was the immoral behavior that took place. What I should have done was work at FedEx as I did, and used the money I made to pay off bills. Instead, I simply added more debt to the pile of debt I already had accumulated.

Having college debt when you graduate is the worst. You get your diploma, you're ready to work (hopefully you get a job soon), but as soon as you start working, most of your check goes to pay for the foolish mistakes you made in college. Learn and live my friend. Not only that but for most graduates, their foolish financial mistakes in college will haunt and stalk them even into their marriage. Schools know how to find you. If you have a school loan, it doesn't matter what part of the world you move to, that yellow document saying it's time to repay your loan will find you. The Postal Service loses mail all the time, except for the student loan bills.

I had a lot of jobs in college. I worked at FedEx, Gold's Gym, a health club on campus, ESPN (assisted the cameramen at football games with their cords), participated in two summer research opportunities programs making $2,500 each summer, and I also worked at Walgreens. Despite all of this, I still graduated with a ton of self-inflicted debt. It didn't have to be like this. I could have saved money by living at home instead of the dorms. I could have worked over the spring break holidays to earn some extra cash. Learn and live, please!

Questions

1. Do you have a checking and savings account? YES/NO. If not, you need to get one.

2. How often do you talk about money? Do you feel comfortable talking about money? If not, why not?

3. Do you currently have any credit cards? How well are you handling them? Are you using a budget? If not, you should.

What to Do

With your finances when you go to college:

- You don't have to go to the most expensive school. If you do, then you will probably have to borrow money. You may want to go to a junior college or a school that will be more feasible to your family's finances. As long as you graduate, it really doesn't matter where you go to school.
- Study what the scriptures have to say about money and debt. Consider the following passages:

  o Genesis 41:1-57.
  o Proverbs 10: 2, 4; 11:4, 28; 13:11; 22:7
  o 1 Timothy 6:6-19.

- You should have no more than one credit card. You don't need five. You probably don't even need a credit card. You should always be able to pay it off within 30 days.
- You don't deserve to go on a spring break trip, buy new gadgets, or brand-new clothes just because everyone else is doing it. You need to

consider how much how all of that will set you back.

- If you can live at home to cut down on costs, then do it. You will have plenty of time to live by yourself when you graduate.

You've Never Drank Alcohol? How Did You Manage That?

by Steven Estes

When I was a boy growing up in Deer Park, Texas, back in the '70s, we had something called blue laws, which my Dad always found difficult because if we needed a part to finish the car repairs on Saturday evening, he was going to have to hitch a ride to work on Monday morning because auto parts were not legal to be sold on Sundays. Most stores, shops, and businesses were required to close on Sundays in the state of Texas so that families could have a day away from work. There were also local ordinances that prevented alcohol from being sold in our city for many years. The blue laws went away in 1985 in Texas. Deer Park began to allow alcohol to be sold, and restaurants in Deer Park were given permission to sell liquor beginning in 2006. Alcohol was seen as something dangerous when I was growing up. Our neighbor across the street would get drunk frequently on the weekends, and his family situation seemed to be a mess because of it. Other neighbors would drink as well, but it was frowned upon. The church where I attended taught that it was wrong to drink alcohol and it seemed that no one ever questioned the idea that drinking alcohol was wrong. Even though some in our community would engage in drinking, they knew it was wrong when they did it. Personally, I have never voluntarily chosen to consume alcohol, which may seem shocking to some in our current decade here in America. The only two times in my life that I have had alcohol in my mouth was as a child by my father's command. When I was about six years old, he forced me at the kitchen sink to take a drink of beer, which I immediately spewed out of my mouth. It tasted nasty, and I had no desire for it at all. He said he wanted me to know what it tasted like so I would never be curious later on and want to drink it. The second time I experienced alcohol was in junior high when Dad forced me to take a sip of white wine at a restaurant. This time I argued, but he demanded strongly that I take a sip. It was not something I preferred, but I think I could have gotten used to the taste of that one. I never could figure out why he had me take that sip, but I always assumed it was for the same reason he had me take the sip of beer. There were some things Dad expected us to do without asking questions, and I sensed this was one of them, so I never asked.

When high school came around, all of my best friends were doing their best to fit in with the crowd. Drinking beer and watching sexually explicit movies was part of that process for them. My friends were seemingly picked off one by one until I became one of the only people I knew in my grade who had not chosen to drink alcohol. There was always one other person I knew who was just like me in this regard and that was my brother Dan who was only one year younger than me. We were close back then and always have been. I admire him for who he is, and he does me too. Who were we? In 9th grade, I had obeyed the gospel and Dan did soon after. We were Christians, and we were bold about our commitment to serve the Lord. Everyone knew we were different: we would not drink alcohol, we never used profanity (not even the words that sounded like profanity), we refused to cheat in school, and we would not attend school dances or participate in things that would be construed as lascivious. Others in my classes, even those who were my best friends at school, would tempt me in various ways to test my resolve to be true to my convictions. I was asked to a party at my best friend's house one Friday night, and I specifically asked him if alcohol would be served at the party. He assured me there would not be any alcohol there, but there would be several girls attending who I was definitely interested in. When I arrived at his house, which was just around the block, I discovered quickly that those showing up to the party were bringing beer of all kinds into the house. I asked my friend where his parents were. He said they were away on a trip. Oh man, this was a recipe for disaster, and I knew it; but everyone had commented about how glad they were to see me at the party since I never came to these kinds of things. I told them I would not have come if I knew there was going to be beer there and my friend's parents were out of town. I asked my friend about why he lied to me about the beer. He said he couldn't control what other people did. I told him that if he did not ask them to take the beer away, then there would be no way I could stay. He refused, so I gathered my jacket and walked back home only having been there for a few minutes. Why did I leave? Because my faith was strong and I did not want to face the idea that I would have violated God's will for my life. I wanted to be a good influence for my best friend in the world as well, my brother Dan. There's no way I could face him if I had violated what we both knew to be wrong. I thought this would be the last time I would face this kind of setup to tempt me to sin, but I was so wrong. My reputation was strong in high school, and everyone knew I could be depended on without reservation because of the stand I held regarding my convictions.

Alcohol was a part of everyone's weekend plans when in high school and college, but I chose not to participate because I knew it was wrong. In college, my reputation was left behind as I attended the University of Houston and became one of tens of thousands of students on the main campus. Here, drinking was expected, and the professors used alcohol as a subject to connect with their students making jokes about it, encouraging it, and sometimes even participating in it with the students. In college, I was seen as an outcast, clueless about real life, and unenlightened. College offered me no support for my faithful convictions, only ridicule. Sometimes, even ridicule in front of the class by the professors. That did not stop me from following God's will and refraining from alcohol.

I married a lovely Christian lady who was literally the answer to my prayers when I was 20 years old, so I was already working full-time when I turned 21 years old, and alcohol was legal for me to drink. All of the people I worked with tried so hard to get me to go with them to drink, but I refused. I could not disappoint my God, and there's no way I could disappoint my wife by violating what we both knew to be wrong. I did not know anyone at work (which was a medical office) that did not drink alcohol and talk about it frequently.

Later on, when I went into medical equipment sales, I was exposed to many people who drank alcohol regularly. Regional Sales Meetings, and especially those in Las Vegas, afforded me the unfortunate opportunity to see many of my peers drunk, except for two individuals. One was a Christian from the Houston area, and another was a Mormon from Arizona. These two guys were such an encouragement to be around because we all knew that we would not be drinking alcohol, carousing with women, and we would be calling our wives each night before bedtime to check on them. I remember one time thinking how isolated I was at the corporate office when we had a team building event, and I was forced to drive the group home because I was the only one who had not had a drink. This was before my two friends joined the company that shared my convictions over alcohol. The refreshing part of that same trip though was what occurred at the National

Sales Award ceremony that year. The CEO of the company I was working for happened to situate himself at my table so we could talk over dinner. When the waiter came by to take my drink order, I told him I would like a glass of tea, and he could take my wine glass because I would not be using it. When the waiter came to the CEO, he told the waiter the same thing. The CEO spoke to me across the table and said if he could have his way about it, he would not serve any alcohol at these dinners, but the management team just won't have it. I always wondered why he didn't just demand they not serve it but thought maybe I didn't understand how the authority worked in the company. He told me he really liked that I didn't drink alcohol and believed I would be more successful than the other guys who did drink. I was the top salesman in the company for three years in a row.

Later when the company I worked for was bought out, the new owners had a very deep alcohol culture, and I was seen as a non-team player for my lack of participation, but behind the scenes, I was highly regarded by the management team. When I resigned from that company, they attempted to retain me, but I knew it wasn't the right fit for me.

When I formed my own company several months later, I disallowed the purchase of alcohol on the company's expense accounts, and we did not serve alcohol at any company function. We eventually sold our company to the largest neurology company in the world, the same company I resigned from eight years earlier…all without the use of alcohol. I never took any of the doctors we served drinking, never took the management team out for drinks, never encouraged drinking in any way.

I have yet to voluntarily consume alcohol and do not ever intend to do so. There are a few lessons I've learned along the way that may be helpful in choosing to abstain from alcohol:

- Remember the commitment you made to God when you became a Christian and don't let anything or anyone intimidate you out of your conviction to do what God has said is right.
- Find others who have made the same commitment and seek to never disappoint them by falling to sin. Imagine the damage you would do to those with the same convictions you have. It could be disastrous not only to you but also to your fellow Christians.

- Marry a Christian spouse who will support your convictions.

- Better understand the word of God in its expectation that we be sober, free from intoxicants. I did not understand this until I was in my mid-30s that God had commanded me to be sober. I had always chosen to refrain from alcohol because I did not want to begin the process of getting drunk because I knew that was forbidden. Understand better what the will of God is for you. It's much easier when we are dealing with what seems to be a black and white rule. Consumption of intoxicating drink is against the will of God, period. I never find myself attempting to find a loophole due to God's vagueness on the matter. It's absolutely wrong, period.

- Convictions must be convictions without wavering, so if you haven't made up your mind on whether you are going to drink alcohol yet, make up your mind now BEFORE you're tempted or encouraged by someone in your life to consume it.

You don't have to drink alcohol to be successful, happily married, or have fun. Trust God no matter what, and the best life that could be will be.

by Keith Stonehart

There is nowhere good to begin my story, and there is no good way to tell it. I'm not a very good writer and yet I determined when I entered ministry that for the glory of God, I would keep nothing back because of the grace of God. If one person could be led to seek His grace because of me telling my story, then I would tell it anytime I am asked.

No matter how embarrassing some of the details of my life are, the truth is that NONE of my story is about me – but about HIM.

"Twas grace that saved a wretch like me."

There a few absolute truths in life:

1. God loves you.
2. God wants you.
3. God has made being with him possible.
4. Satan will do everything he can to keep you from believing the first 3 are true.

Another truth about Satan is that he will not wait for you to grow up to come after you.

He will come after you young.

The first time I drank alcohol I was 9 years old. Like many nine-year-olds, part of the draw was curiosity, but more than that I was seeking a way to stop feeling. You might think of that as a heavy thought for a nine-year-old, but for the four previous years, I had been sexually molested by an older family member. By the age of nine, I had figured out that what had been happening to me was not normal or okay as I had been told.

I had been lied to… and I had been hurt. There was shame, confusion, anger, and frustration to say the least and to only name a few of the emotions that had been awakened in me, and my young nine-year-old mind was looking for an escape.

By 14, I had graduated to pot and LSD. By 16, cocaine. When I graduated high school, I was a full-blown, full-functioning addict.

To fuel the fire, I had started a rock band during high school, and despite our appetite for excess and destruction, we were a really good band and had already become very popular in the growing Atlanta music scene. After catching the attention of a well-known manager and booking company, we began to tour the country right after graduation. We were four misfit boys now thrown into a very adult world and rigorous touring schedule that included excess of every variety.

By 24, Satan had full sway over me. The drugs, parties, and women had worn my sensibilities to a dull state of apathy. What little belief in God I may have had as a child was all but gone. My cynicism had callused me, and my mind was bent... and then I met Kelly.

She was good.

There is no other way to describe the woman that would eventually become my wife. There was a goodness and a morality about her that was completely foreign to me and also very attractive to me. I couldn't quite put my finger on it, but she was truly different.

We began to date, and slowly but surely, she began to break through my calloused layers. Though my partying had slowed down, it had not stopped. Even after we were married two years later, I continued to use secretly. Binging on the weekends when the band would play shows regionally. We had stopped touring, but still played every weekend, which seemed to satisfy my need, for a while anyway. Like everything else, however, time had a way of working on me and Satan knew it, and before long, the binging began again.

After the birth of my daughter, I began to question my lifestyle. I was beginning to realize that I couldn't carry on the way I was if I intended to be any sort of father. My father was an abusive addict himself and the very kind of man that I swore I'd never become—and yet, there I was.

Just like him.

I also had begun to question my atheism. Witnessing the birth of my daughter had a very profound and unexpected effect on me. Couple that with Kelly's family and their desire to share their faith with me at every turn, I began to see that maybe, just maybe there was a God—but surely—He wanted nothing to do with me. I was damaged goods, too far gone and unlovable. I was convinced if He was real that He must have hated me. The lies of the enemy had become my truth, and objective truth seemed out of my grasp. I continued to spiral downward until all my binging caught up with me.

The other women, the drugs, the lies—Enough.

Kelly had enough, and she left. She took my daughter, and they left me on October 1, 2001.

When I got home to my empty house, I couldn't help but see the irony in the emptiness the house represented in myself. Truly believing that my life was over, I gathered every bit of cocaine I had and decided I would begin to snort myself into a state where I couldn't feel the hurt that I was feeling, maybe ever again. Just as I was about to begin, my doorbell rang.

It was Mark, my brother-in-law.

He insisted that he wouldn't stay long and that he just wanted to check on me. Kelly had gone to his house, and so he knew everything that was going on with us.

"What are you doing, man" he asked.

I had no answer.

After a very long pause and trying to find any words that could make sense of my mess, I finally began to speak. For the next 3 hours, I then told my brother-in-law every ugly truth about me.

I told him everything, things I had never told anyone. Things I had pushed way down inside. It was as if 28 years of pain was beginning to lift from my heart. All the while he just listened. When I was finally done, there was a long silence. It seemed like an eternity, though maybe just a few minutes in reality.

My mind raced. I wondered what he was going to say. I imagined that he would judge me, tell me that I deserved to be alone, but no.

He began to pray.

I was stunned. Awkwardly moved, but stunned.

"You know I don't believe in that," I said.

"But I do," Mark replied.

"No one has ever prayed for me," I said.

"Not true, my wife and I pray for you every day," he said.

"Really? What do you Y'all pray for?" I asked.

"This opportunity."

He went on to explain his wife (Kelly's sister) was back at his house having this same conversation with Kelly and that they had been wanting to share their faith with us. They had seen the damage the world was doing to us but never seemed to find the right opportunity to start the conversation.

He went on to share with me that there is, in fact, a God. Not only could he prove to me that He was real, but also that He loved me, that He did want me, and that I WAS NOT TOO FAR GONE.

It sounded too good to be true, but he had my attention none the less.

So, I agreed to go to his church with him, and since I agreed to go, he would do his best to persuade Kelly to meet me there also. He did, and she came.

I was scared to death walking in that building. Again, I was waiting for the stares and the judgments and yet, much to my surprise, there were none. There only seemed to be people who were very excited and happy to see me. They didn't seem to care about my appearance or whatever emotional baggage I had in tow. They only seemed to care that we were there and that we mattered.

The preacher there was a big man named Brownie. He was tall and white-headed and seemed to be very intimidating at first until he spoke. His face lit up and when he introduced himself and even more so when he asked if we would like to study the Bible with him. I told him I didn't have one to which he responded: "Here, take this one" and gave me the one he was holding. "I'll bring another one for me tomorrow night. What's your address?"

And just like that, we began to study the Bible the very next night.

Brownie let me ask all of my gotcha questions— the things that I thought I knew about the Bible and God and how I might be able to stump him with my vast worldly knowledge, and yet every single time he answered from his Bible. The impression this made on me was HUGE. Could this book really be the word of God? Could this mean that God was real and that He did love me? He did want me? That I was NOT too far gone?

No doubt, Satan wanted to keep me, and the spiritual warfare was elevated as my mind began to open up to the word of God and I began to listen to it.

I was beginning to believe.

At this point, we confided in Brownie all that we were dealing with—my addiction, adultery, dishonesty, pornography—ALL of it. He listened patiently, and though he never pulled any punches, he never hit me with cheap shots regarding my behavior but rather explained the biblical view of them.

Two weeks later, on November 12, 2001, Kelly and I were baptized for the remission of our sins.

The next 5 years would be the most difficult years of my life. Overcoming addiction, overcoming adultery in my marriage, leaving an entire lifestyle and group of friends behind, and learning a new and better way to live in service to the King. Satan fought for me, sometimes winning, but more and more when I would resist, he would flee, just like the Bible said he would.

In spite of the devil's pursuit of us and his mission to keep us captive we grew. We studied the Bible daily as a couple, we studied weekly with Brownie, and we studied and participated in every study going on outside of worship that we could, along with Bible classes at church. We just soaked it in.

I was asked to preach on April 5, 2009, for the first time at the Lanier church of Christ in Buford, Georgia. From then going forward I would preach regularly a couple of times per month for the next 3 years until moving to Fultondale, Alabama, to preach fulltime in October 2012 where I am currently still serving the Lord in that role.

Here is what I have learned.

There a few absolute truths in life and they are the same that I began this story with:

1. God loves you.
2. God wants you.
3. God has made being with Him possible.
4. Satan will do everything he can to keep you from believing the first three are true.

I wish that I could convey just how very true these four points are. Even in telling you what all the

Lord has delivered me through in the last 18 years still doesn't quite capture the fervor in which I believe these four truths.

And I know this also—whatever your circumstance— you can overcome through Him who overcame the world. The hard work of salvation has already been done by Christ so take comfort in that, but the work of discipleship will be up to you.

Read.

Study.

Believe.

Meditate.

Practice.

Repeat.

John 16:33, "These things I have spoken to you, so that in Me you have peace. In the world you have tribulation, but take courage; I have overcome the world."

God loves you, and so do I.

Moral Decision-Making

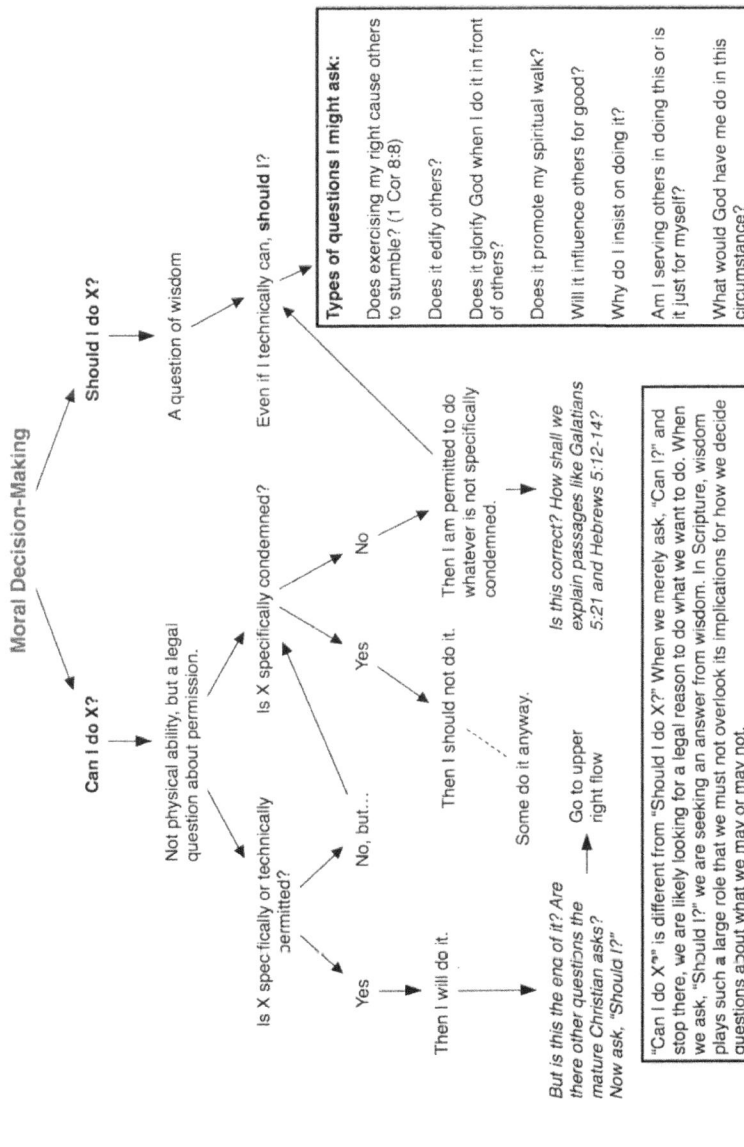

Moral Decision-Making

Can I do X?

Should I do X?

A question of wisdom

Not physical ability, but a legal question about permission.

Even if I technically can, **should** I?

Types of questions I might ask:

Does exercising my right cause others to stumble? (1 Cor 8:8)

Does it edify others?

Does it glorify God when I do it in front of others?

Does it promote my spiritual walk?

Will it influence others for good?

Why do I insist on doing it?

Am I serving others in doing this or is it just for myself?

What would God have me do in this circumstance?

Is X specifically or technically permitted?

Is X specifically condemned?

Yes

No, but...

Yes

No

Then I will do it.

Then I should not do it.

Then I am permitted to do whatever is not specifically condemned.

Some do it anyway.

Go to upper right flow

Then I should do it.

Is this correct? How shall we explain passages like Galatians 5:21 and Hebrews 5:12-14?

But is this the end of it? Are there other questions the mature Christian asks? Now ask, "Should I?"

"Can I do X?" is different from "Should I do X?" When we merely ask, "Can I?" and stop there, we are likely looking for a legal reason to do what we want to do. When we ask, "Should I?" we are seeking an answer from wisdom. In Scripture, wisdom plays such a large role that we must not overlook its implications for how we decide questions about what we may or may not.

Doy Moyer

Conclusion

I'm sure there's more I could say in this book, but I wanted to keep it short. I hope you have learned something from my mistakes. I hope you are encouraged to listen to the Bible more and to trust in God. As you begin a new journey of life, I want you to consider Joshua 1:1-8. I want you to read this text often. Just as Joshua was facing a new land, so are you as you begin college. Just like Joshua, you can be successful. But you will have to fully trust in the Lord. Just like Joshua, you will have enemies you will have to face. But always remember the God of Abraham, Isaac, and Jacob is with you. Trust Him!

Learn and live, my friend.

—Benjamin Lee

Made in the USA
Coppell, TX
30 April 2025

48843083R00036